Spider Girl

Written by
Cath Jones

Illustrated by
Suzanne Washington

Jade looked at the large black spider on the wheel of her chair.

"Good morning, Seth!" she said.

Seth began to spin a web.

Spiders' webs hung from every corner of Jade's bedroom. The sunshine made them glitter. They looked delightful.

"It's the school fancy dress party today," Jade said. "I would like to go very much, but I have nothing to wear."

Seth ran up his web to chat to the other spiders.

"We need to help Jade," he said.

"How can **we** help?" they asked. "We are only little spiders!"

But Seth knew just what to do. "We may be little, but our webs are big," he said.

Soon, all the bedroom spiders began to spin.

They spun webs with fancy patterns and long, graceful ribbons.

They made a wonderful fancy dress outfit for Jade.

When Jade saw the fancy dress costume, she was astonished.

"Oh thank you!" she said. "It's so delicate! It's the best costume I have ever seen."

But it had taken the spiders so long to make it that it was nearly time for the party to begin!

"How will I get to the party on time?" Jade asked Seth. "I don't have a pumpkin to turn into a coach!"

"Don't worry," said Seth. "I have a plan!"

The spiders set to work.

They spun a very long, strong bridge for Jade. It went all the way from her bedroom window to the school playground.

"Wow!" said Jade.

All the spiders got onto her shoulders.

"Hang on tight," she said.

Whizz! Jade shot off down the bridge. It was great fun!

When Jade went into the party, all the children looked at her in shock.

Jade had the best fancy dress costume they had ever seen!

Then they laughed, because everyone knew that Jade was a big fan of spiders!

The music at the party was terrific. Jade, Seth, the spiders and everybody else spun round and round together.

It was so much fun.

Seth made a fancy bonnet for Jade and a huge wig for Jade's teacher. Everyone laughed.

The spiders were a huge hit!

At the end of the party, the headteacher called for hush.

It was time to judge who had the best fancy dress costume.

She looked at all the fancy dress outfits. Which one would she choose?

"The winner," she said …

… is Jade and the spiders!"